I0020106

Gemini Unveiled

Navigating Human-AI Fusion, from Coding
Prowess to Offline Brilliance – Explore
Google's Multimodal Revolution

Tech Talker

All rights reserved. No part of this publication may be reproduced, distributed, or transmitted in any form or by any means, including photocopying, recording, or other electronic or mechanical methods, without the prior written permission of the publisher, except in the case of brief quotations embodied in critical reviews and certain other noncommercial uses permitted by copyright law.

Copyright © Tech Talker, 2023.

Table of contents

Introduction...3

Chapter 1:...6

The Genesis of Gemini..........................6

Chapter 2:..15

Gemini's Expertise.................................. 15

Chapter 3:..30

Coding Revolution with AlphaCode 2...................... 30

Chapter 4:..37

Behind the Scenes: Training on Tensor Processing Units...37

Chapter 5:..43

Variants of Gemini.................................. 43

Chapter 6:..49

Integrating Gemini with Bard.................. 49

Chapter 7:..60

Using Google Gemini on Pixel 8 Pro...................... 60

Chapter 8:..65

Limitations and Future Prospects........................... 65

Conclusion..70

Introduction

Embark on a thrilling odyssey into the heart of the AI revolution, where Google's newest marvel, Gemini, emerges as a beacon of innovation. We're not just diving into the complexities of a language model; we're venturing into the uncharted territories of artificial intelligence that Gemini boldly navigates.

Picture this: Gemini AI, a symphony that transcends the limits of conventional language processing. It's not merely a model; it's a visionary force that sweeps across computer vision, geospatial science, human health, and integrated technologies. It's the conductor orchestrating a revolutionary landscape in artificial intelligence.

Gemini is not satisfied with the ordinary; it craves the extraordinary. This book is your backstage pass to witness the birth of a multimodal maestro. Text, images, video, audio, and code dance in harmony, setting the stage for a performance that defies expectations.

Chapter 1:

The Genesis of Gemini

In the fast-evolving landscape of artificial intelligence, Google's latest venture, Gemini, has emerged as a cutting-edge large language model. This chapter delves into the origins and purpose behind Gemini, providing a comprehensive understanding of its inception.

Gemini didn't materialize overnight; it was born from a collective vision to push the boundaries of AI. Conceived by a team of visionary engineers and data scientists at Google, Gemini represents a significant leap forward in language modeling.

The driving force behind Gemini lies in addressing the shortcomings of conventional language processing models. Google envisioned a model that could seamlessly integrate text, images, video, audio, and code—a multimodal AI that transcends the limitations of its predecessors.

Gemini's journey from concept to reality involved meticulous planning and technological innovation. It underwent iterative development, with each stage refining its capabilities and expanding its scope. The model's evolution reflects a commitment to staying at the forefront of AI advancements.

At its core, Gemini is not just a technological feat; it's a purpose-driven creation with the goal of reshaping how we interact with AI. By excelling in computer vision, geospatial science, human health, and integrated technologies, Gemini aims to be a versatile solution to diverse real-world challenges.

Behind the scenes, a team of brilliant minds collaborated to bring Gemini to life. Engineers, researchers, and visionaries worked in unison, leveraging their expertise to create a model that goes beyond conventional language understanding.

Gemini's capabilities are grounded in advanced algorithms and the utilization of Tensor Processing Units (TPUs). These technological foundations empower Gemini with speed, efficiency, and the ability to handle large-scale tasks.

As we uncover the genesis of Gemini, we set the stage for a journey into the intricate workings of this multifaceted AI model. The purpose, vision, and collaborative efforts that birthed Gemini lay the groundwork for the exploration that follows—a journey into the future of artificial intelligence.

In the ever-expanding universe of artificial intelligence, Google's Gemini stands as a trailblazer in the realm of multimodal capabilities. This section delves into the remarkable prowess of Gemini, showcasing its seamless processing of text, images, video, audio, and code.

Gemini's mastery begins with text, where it exhibits a nuanced understanding and processing of language. Whether deciphering complex sentences or generating contextually rich responses, Gemini sets a new standard in textual intelligence.

The integration of computer vision capabilities elevates Gemini to unprecedented heights. Object detection, scene understanding, and anomaly detection become second nature to Gemini as it effortlessly interprets and analyzes visual information.

Gemini's foray into video processing extends its reach across dynamic and temporal data. Scene-by-scene analysis, action recognition, and content summarization become part of Gemini's cinematic prowess, revolutionizing how AI interacts with video content.

In the realm of audio, Gemini demonstrates a unique ability to interpret and respond to spoken words. Its proficiency spans from transcription accuracy to nuanced understanding of tones, inflections, and accents, making it a versatile player in audio-based interactions.

A standout feature of Gemini lies in its prowess with code. AlphaCode 2, Gemini's code-generating system, takes center stage, outperforming human participants in coding competitions. Whether it's generating snippets or providing solutions, Gemini's coding capabilities redefine the landscape.

What sets Gemini apart is its ability to seamlessly weave together these modalities. Text, images, video, audio, and code converge to create a unified, comprehensive understanding. Gemini's multimodal mastery transcends siloed approaches, offering a holistic and nuanced interaction with diverse types of data.

The applications of Gemini's multimodal capabilities extend across various domains. From enhancing healthcare diagnostics with image and biosensor integration to transforming decision-making processes with integrated technologies, Gemini leaves an indelible mark on real-world scenarios.

As we unravel the layers of Gemini's multimodal mastery, we catch a glimpse of the future—a future where AI seamlessly integrates with our diverse ways of communication and understanding.

Chapter 2:

Gemini's Expertise

In the intricate tapestry of Gemini's capabilities, its prowess in computer vision takes center stage. This chapter is a deep dive into Gemini's extraordinary capacities in object detection, scene understanding, and anomaly detection—ushering in a new era of visual intelligence.

Gemini's mastery in object detection is a testament to its unrivaled precision. Whether identifying everyday objects or navigating complex scenes, Gemini's algorithms work seamlessly to recognize and categorize visual elements with unparalleled accuracy.

Beyond recognizing individual objects, Gemini possesses an innate understanding of entire scenes. It interprets the context, relationships, and interactions within a visual landscape, providing a level of scene understanding that transcends conventional computer vision models.

Gemini's capabilities extend to anomaly detection, making it a guardian in the visual realm. By discerning irregularities and deviations from expected patterns, Gemini becomes an invaluable tool in various domains, from security to quality control.

What sets Gemini apart is its dynamic adaptability in real-time scenarios. Whether in a bustling cityscape, a medical environment, or an industrial setting, Gemini adapts its object detection, scene understanding, and anomaly detection in a manner that aligns with the specific demands of each context.

The real-world applications of Gemini's computer vision prowess are far-reaching. From optimizing traffic flow in smart cities to enhancing surveillance systems with anomaly detection, Gemini's visual intelligence finds practical implementation in diverse domains.

As we navigate through Gemini's capabilities in computer vision, we witness a transformative impact on how AI interprets and interacts with the visual world. Gemini's precision and adaptability lay the foundation for a future where computer vision transcends limitations, offering a more nuanced understanding of our surroundings.

Gemini's influence expands into the intricate domain of geospatial science, revolutionizing our understanding of the world. By seamlessly fusing data from diverse sources, Gemini orchestrates a harmonious blend of multisource information, creating a unified perspective that transcends traditional boundaries.

In the realm of geospatial intelligence, Gemini doesn't just process data—it becomes a strategic ally in planning and decision-making. From urban development projects to disaster response initiatives, Gemini's algorithms contribute a layer of intelligent insights, shaping a more informed and proactive approach to spatial challenges.

Continuous monitoring, a cornerstone of geospatial science, is elevated to new heights with Gemini. Its vigilant eye tracks environmental shifts, monitors critical infrastructure, and oversees dynamic urban landscapes. The result is a constant flow of relevant, real-time information that forms the foundation for adaptive responses to emerging scenarios.

Gemini's adaptability extends beyond mere observation; it actively responds to geospatial insights. By interpreting patterns and changes in the environment, Gemini empowers decision-makers with the tools to proactively address challenges, ensuring a more resilient and responsive approach to a dynamic world.

The impact of Gemini's geospatial prowess reverberates through practical applications. Resource optimization in smart cities, disaster preparedness strategies, and the ability to respond swiftly to unfolding events are just a few examples of how Gemini's geospatial intelligence reshapes our interaction with the physical world.

What sets Gemini apart is not just its geospatial mastery in isolation but its ability to synergize with other modalities. By integrating geospatial data with visual and textual information, Gemini creates a comprehensive understanding that goes beyond individual data types, opening new avenues for richer insights and more sophisticated applications.

As we immerse ourselves in Gemini's geospatial capabilities, it becomes evident that we are on the brink of a geospatially intelligent future.

Gemini's transformative influence extends into the realm of human health, where it emerges as a catalyst for innovation in personalized healthcare, biosensor integration, and preventative medicine. In this chapter, we unravel the impact of Gemini's applications in the vital domain of healthcare.

Gemini spearheads a revolution in healthcare by ushering in the era of personalized medicine. Its advanced understanding of diverse health data enables tailored and targeted approaches to patient care, ensuring treatments align with individual needs, genetic makeup, and lifestyle factors.

Gemini seamlessly integrates with biosensors, amplifying its capabilities in health monitoring. By interfacing with biosensors, Gemini enables real-time data collection, offering a holistic view of an individual's health metrics. This integration paves the way for more accurate diagnostics and personalized health interventions.

In the realm of preventative medicine, Gemini acts as a proactive guardian of health. Its analytical prowess interprets patterns and risk factors, allowing for early detection of potential health issues. By emphasizing preventative measures, Gemini contributes to a shift in healthcare paradigms from reactive to proactive.

Gemini's capabilities shine in diagnostics, where its nuanced understanding of medical data aids in precise and swift diagnoses. From medical imaging to analyzing clinical reports, Gemini's accuracy enhances the diagnostic process, leading to more effective and timely interventions.

The real-world impact of Gemini's applications in human health is profound. Patients experience more personalized treatment plans, improved monitoring of chronic conditions, and early interventions that enhance overall well-being. Gemini's contributions extend to a healthcare landscape that prioritizes individual needs and preventative measures.

As we explore Gemini's role in healthcare, we also delve into the ethical considerations that arise. From data privacy concerns to ensuring equitable access to personalized healthcare, Gemini prompts important conversations about the responsible and ethical implementation of advanced AI technologies in the healthcare sector.

This chapter is not just about Gemini's current applications; it's about envisioning a future where healthcare is truly personalized, preventative, and technologically advanced. Join us in navigating the transformative landscape of healthcare, where Gemini plays a pivotal role in reshaping the way we approach human well-being.

Gemini's influence transcends individual domains, converging in a symphony of integrated technologies. In this chapter, we unravel the intricate synergy of domain knowledge transfer, data fusion, enhanced decision-making, and the pivotal role of large language models in shaping a new era of technological integration.

Gemini serves as a bridge, transferring knowledge seamlessly across diverse domains. Its ability to adapt and understand specialized knowledge domains facilitates a fluid exchange of insights, fostering collaboration and innovation across traditionally siloed sectors.

At the heart of integrated technologies lies Gemini's prowess in data fusion. It harmonizes information from disparate sources, creating a unified and comprehensive dataset. This fusion not only enhances the accuracy of insights but also opens avenues for discovering correlations and patterns previously hidden in individual datasets.

Gemini's impact on decision-making is transformative. By providing nuanced insights and contextual understanding, Gemini empowers decision-makers to navigate complex scenarios with a heightened level of clarity. The integration of large language models contributes to more informed and data-driven decision processes.

Large language models, a forte of Gemini, act as the linguistic backbone of integrated technologies. Their advanced language understanding, generation capabilities, and contextual reasoning enhance communication, knowledge transfer, and decision-making across a spectrum of applications.

The real-world applications of integrated technologies powered by Gemini are diverse. From optimizing supply chain management through enhanced decision-making to revolutionizing customer interactions through language models, Gemini's influence permeates various sectors, bringing about a paradigm shift in how technologies collaborate.

As we delve into the synergies of integrated technologies, we address ethical considerations and challenges. Issues of data privacy, responsible AI use, and the potential biases inherent in large language models prompt a critical examination of the ethical dimensions of integrated technologies.

Chapter 3:

Coding Revolution with AlphaCode

2

In the dynamic realm of coding, Google's AlphaCode 2 emerges as a transformative force, pushing the boundaries of what's possible in code generation. This chapter takes you on a journey into the heart of AlphaCode 2, revealing its innovative prowess and exceptional performance in coding competitions.

AlphaCode 2 is the result of Google's commitment to advancing code generation. Building on the success of its predecessor, AlphaCode 1, this iteration introduces groundbreaking improvements, setting a new standard in the world of code creation.

Beyond being a mere code generator, AlphaCode 2 is a virtuoso in crafting solutions. Its capabilities surpass those of human participants, showcasing remarkable proficiency in solving complex algorithms and generating sophisticated code.

AlphaCode 2 doesn't just participate in coding competitions; it excels, standing as a testament to the next level of achievement in competitive coding.

Building upon the foundations laid by AlphaCode 1, AlphaCode 2 introduces key advancements that elevate its performance, reinforcing its position as a cutting-edge code-generating system.

AlphaCode 2 seamlessly integrates with Gemini, Google's large language model, forming a powerful synergy that extends their impact beyond coding competitions to broader applications.

AlphaCode 2's impact extends to real-world applications, contributing to addressing practical coding challenges, aiding software development, and automating repetitive coding tasks.

Innovation is not without challenges. This chapter addresses the hurdles faced by AlphaCode 2, from mitigating biases in code generation to ensuring ethical use. Additionally, it offers insights into anticipated future developments, paving the way for the continuous evolution of Google's code-generating marvel.

In the dynamic realm of coding, Gemini emerges as a transformative force, redefining coding experiences and leaving an indelible mark across various applications.

Gemini transcends conventional coding boundaries, ushering in a new era where developers engage with their craft intuitively. Enhanced coding experiences redefine the developer's journey.

Beyond its coding core, Gemini's influence extends seamlessly across applications, optimizing workflows, and automating coding tasks with remarkable versatility.

Gemini's multimodal prowess, processing text, images, video, audio, and code, introduces a holistic coding approach that breaks traditional barriers, transforming how developers conceptualize and implement code.

The integration of Gemini with AlphaCode 2 amplifies coding efficiency, creating a dynamic synergy that streamlines processes and fosters creativity in code generation.

Gemini's impact on software development is tangible, accelerating timelines and contributing to the creation of robust and efficient software solutions in the real world.

Gemini serves as a collaborative bridge, facilitating seamless communication and knowledge transfer among developers with different expertise, transcending traditional coding silos.

As coding evolves with Gemini, ethical considerations take center stage, addressing implications such as unbiased code generation and promoting responsible AI practices.

Looking forward, this section explores the potential horizons of Gemini in coding, envisioning how it will continue to revolutionize the developer experience and shape the future of coding practices.

Chapter 4:

Behind the Scenes: Training on Tensor Processing Units

At the heart of Gemini's evolution lies the Tensor Processing Unit (TPU), a powerhouse that catapults its training into unprecedented realms of speed and cost-effectiveness.

TPUs redefine speed in machine learning. Gemini's training on TPU accelerates the learning curve, setting a new standard for large language models.

TPU architecture transforms the training process, pushing Gemini's capabilities to new heights and redefining the speed of large language models.

Training on TPU not only accelerates but also optimizes costs. Gemini's training on

TPU outperforms its predecessors, delivering both speed and cost-effectiveness.

Gemini's training on TPU is a dual triumph—faster and more cost-effective. This section explores the efficiency gained, making Gemini an economical large language model.

The synergy of Gemini and TPU goes beyond speed, enhancing the overall model efficiency. TPU's architecture contributes significantly to refining Gemini's capabilities.

Gemini's TPU-trained model has tangible implications across applications. From expedited model deployment to real-time processing efficiency, this chapter showcases the transformative impact on diverse use cases.

Embark on this exploration of TPU's pivotal role in Gemini's training revolution, where speed and cost-effectiveness converge to redefine the possibilities of large language models.

TPU v5p, the latest gem in Google's Tensor Processing Unit series, redefines the game in large-scale model processing. This chapter unpacks the brilliance of TPU v5p's architecture, a testament to engineering ingenuity that powers unparalleled efficiency in handling mammoth models.

In the realm of precision and acceleration, TPU v5p doesn't just break barriers; it obliterates them. This section peels back the curtain on how TPU v5p's advanced design doesn't just speed up large-scale model training and execution; it sets an entirely new standard for what's possible.

Optimized explicitly for scale, TPU v5p isn't intimidated by complexity. It's built to handle the big leagues, seamlessly navigating the intricate demands of large language models. Scalability isn't a challenge; it's a feature, making TPU v5p a transformative force in efficient model processing.

Applications across domains showcase TPU v5p's versatility. Whether it's language models or cutting-edge computer vision tasks, TPU v5p doesn't discriminate.

Real-world examples unfold, highlighting its impact in diverse fields that hunger for swift, efficient large-scale model processing.

Gazing into the crystal ball, we ponder the future TPU v5p ushers in for large-scale model processing. The speculations in this section are more than educated guesses; they're an invitation to envision the next chapter in the dynamic saga of machine learning innovation.

Chapter 5:

Variants of Gemini

Gemini, Google's latest large language model, comes in three distinct variants tailored to meet diverse user needs and tasks. Let's explore each variant and uncover the unique features they bring to the table.

Nano: Fast On-Device Powerhouse

Nano, designed for on-the-fly tasks, packs a punch in a compact form. Users can experience rapid on-device interactions, making Nano the ideal choice for quick, efficient responses without sacrificing performance.

Pro: Versatile Middle Tier

Pro, the middle-tier variant, is the epitome of versatility. Its advanced text-based capabilities make it suitable for a wide range of applications. From information retrieval to creative endeavors, Pro adapts seamlessly to cater to varied user requirements.

Ultra: The Pinnacle of Power

Ultra, the powerhouse of the trio, is currently undergoing safety checks for a future release. Anticipated to be available next year (2024), Ultra promises to be a game-changer for high-performance tasks and intensive operations. It represents the pinnacle of Gemini, offering maximum power and capabilities.

Embark on this exploration of the Gemini variants, where Nano, Pro, and Ultra cater to a spectrum of user needs, ensuring that Gemini aligns seamlessly with diverse tasks and preferences.

How Gemini's efficiency surpasses its predecessor, PaLM.

In the evolution of large language models, efficiency marks a pivotal milestone. PaLM, Google's predecessor to Gemini, set the stage, but it faced challenges. Gemini emerges as a transformative leap, redefining efficiency in large-scale language models.

PaLM, while foundational, struggled with speed and cost-effectiveness. Its limitations paved the way for Gemini's innovation, creating an imperative shift in the efficiency paradigm.

Gemini's efficiency breakthrough lies in its training methodology. Trained on Google's

Tensor Processing Units (TPUs), it achieves enhanced speed and cost-effectiveness, addressing the shortcomings of PaLM. This section unveils the technical prowess behind Gemini's efficiency.

The comparison is stark—Gemini outpaces PaLM in both speed and cost-effectiveness. This part dissects the advantages, illustrating the tangible efficiency gains that Gemini brings to the table, setting a new standard for large language models.

The chapter concludes with a glimpse into the future—TPU v5p. This upcoming iteration promises an even more efficient era for Gemini, pushing the boundaries of speed, cost-effectiveness, and overall performance. The efficiency journey continues with anticipation for what lies ahead.

Embark on this exploration into efficiency unleashed by Gemini, where it not only outshines PaLM but sets a new benchmark, ensuring a seamless and enhanced experience for users of large language models.

Chapter 6:

Integrating Gemini with Bard

In the ever-evolving landscape of artificial intelligence, Bard, Google's chatbot, stands as a testament to the seamless integration of innovation and user-centric design. This chapter traces Bard's captivating journey from its inception to the groundbreaking integration with Gemini, unlocking new realms of advanced reasoning and understanding.

Bard was born out of the vision to create a chatbot that not only engages in conversations but also masters the art of information retrieval. Its early days were characterized by a commitment to user-friendly interactions and context-aware responses.

As Bard gained traction, its capabilities grew. Natural language processing became a forte, and Bard distinguished itself by providing users with an intuitive and contextually relevant conversational experience. These early strides paved the way for what was to come.

The narrative takes a transformative turn as Bard integrates with Gemini, Google's revolutionary large language model. This integration marks a paradigm shift in the capabilities of chatbots. Gemini's advanced reasoning and understanding elevate Bard to new heights, setting it apart in the competitive landscape of conversational AI.

The synergy of Bard and Gemini reshapes the user experience. With advanced reasoning at its core, Bard now generates responses with unparalleled accuracy and quality. Users find themselves engaged in conversations that feel more natural and tailored to their intents.

The chapter concludes by hinting at the future – a future where Bard's capabilities expand into the realm of multimodal interactions. With Bard Advanced powered by Gemini Ultra on the horizon, users can anticipate a seamless fusion of text, images, audio, and video, ushering in a new era of interactive possibilities.

Embark on this journey through Bard's evolution, where each phase unfolds with a commitment to innovation, user satisfaction, and the relentless pursuit of excellence in the world of conversational AI.

How Gemini enhances Bard's ability to generate accurate, high-quality responses

In the realm of conversational AI, Gemini, Google's latest large language model, revolutionizes how Bard responds to user queries. This chapter unravels the impact of Gemini on Bard's ability to elevate the precision of responses, ensuring accuracy and quality that redefine user interactions.

Understanding User Intent:
Gemini acts as the cognitive powerhouse, enabling Bard to delve deep into user intent. By harnessing Gemini's advanced language understanding, Bard transcends traditional

chatbot limitations, deciphering nuanced user queries with unparalleled accuracy.

Precision Unleashed:

The marriage of Bard with Gemini is a game-changer, unlocking a new standard of precision. Gemini's multimodal capabilities empower Bard to not only comprehend text intricacies but also integrate insights from images, audio, and video, crafting responses that surpass expectations.

Contextual Awareness Elevated:

Gemini elevates Bard's contextual awareness to new heights. Beyond standalone responses, Bard, infused with Gemini's capabilities, weaves context seamlessly into conversations. The result is a more natural and engaging user experience that adapts to the nuances of ongoing dialogue.

Navigating Ambiguity:

Ambiguity in language poses no challenge with Gemini in the mix. This section explores how Gemini's robust reasoning equips Bard to navigate through ambiguous queries, ensuring clarity and relevance in responses, irrespective of the intricacies of user input.

User-Centric Conversations:

Gemini isn't just a technological upgrade; it's a catalyst for user-centric conversations. Discover how Gemini transforms Bard's responses, aligning them with user needs and preferences. The result is a dynamic and meaningful interaction that resonates with users on a deeper level.

Embark on this journey through enhanced responses, where Gemini's prowess reshapes the conversational landscape. Precision, contextual awareness, and user-centricity converge to deliver a transformative experience, marking a new era in the evolution of conversational AI.

The future of human-AI interaction with Gemini's multimodal capabilities

Gemini's revolutionary multimodal capabilities are reshaping the landscape of human-AI interaction, offering a glimpse into a future where communication transcends traditional boundaries.

The Rise of Multimodality:

Gemini introduces a paradigm shift by seamlessly integrating text, images, audio, and video. This evolution goes beyond words, providing users with a more immersive and holistic interaction with AI.

Text Meets Visuals:

Gemini's fusion of text and visuals creates a dynamic synergy. Real-world examples demonstrate how this integration enhances communication, offering a richer and more nuanced understanding of information.

Enriching Conversations with Audio:

Gemini transforms conversations by introducing audio elements. From natural-sounding responses to the incorporation of audio cues, this addition adds depth and a new layer of engagement to the interactive experience.

The Visual Impact:

Visual elements take on a pivotal role as Gemini enhances the conveyance and comprehension of information. Discover how visuals, once supplementary, now play a central role in influencing user engagement and understanding.

A Symphony of Modalities:

Gemini orchestrates a seamless symphony, harmonizing text, images, audio, and video.

This convergence paints a vivid picture of a future where these modalities work together, offering users a comprehensive and immersive interaction with AI.

Chapter 7:

Using Google Gemini on Pixel 8 Pro

Gemini Nano introduces a game-changing dimension to your Pixel 8 Pro by operating offline. Its lean design ensures a seamless and responsive user experience, free from the constraints of constant internet connectivity.

Explore how Gemini Nano redefines communication even without an internet link. Your Pixel 8 Pro becomes an intelligent conversationalist, offering relevant and natural responses in messaging apps, ensuring your interactions remain dynamic and contextually aware offline.

Gemini Nano extends its capabilities to the Recorder app, enabling instant audio summarization with a tap. Efficiently obtain brief overviews of your recordings, showcasing the adaptability of Gemini Nano, even in offline environments.

Immerse yourself in the enhanced features of Gemini Nano offline on the Pixel 8 Pro. Smart Reply and Recorder functionalities continue to thrive, providing a feature-rich experience regardless of your connection status.

Smart Reply and Recorder functionalities powered by Gemini Nano

Gemini Nano transforms your Pixel 8 Pro's Smart Reply into a dynamic communicator. Experience contextually relevant and natural responses, witnessing the evolution of Smart Reply.

Explore Gemini Nano's impact on the Recorder app, streamlining your recording management. Generate quick overviews with a tap, enhancing efficiency in summarization.

Discover Gemini Nano's seamless intelligence in offline scenarios. Smart Reply remains responsive and intelligent, ensuring uninterrupted communication. The Recorder app generates summaries offline, offering flexibility.

Gemini Nano enhances online and offline interactions. Smart Reply and Recorder functionalities thrive, delivering a feature-rich experience. Dive into the versatility of Gemini Nano, adapting to dynamic needs.

Experience the next level of convenience and intelligence as Gemini Nano powers up Smart Reply and Recorder functionalities on your Pixel 8 Pro. From messaging to recording management, Gemini Nano ensures a seamless and enriched user experience.

Chapter 8:

Limitations and Future Prospects

Gemini Pro's integration within Bard is currently limited to English-only interactions. This limitation hinders global accessibility, creating a barrier for users who prefer languages other than English.

As of now, Gemini Pro's integration in Bard has not been introduced in the European Union (EU). This geographical constraint limits the availability and reach of Gemini Pro's capabilities within Bard.

Gemini Pro within Bard is currently limited to text-based interactions. While its capabilities are extensive, the absence of multimodal features in this integration leaves users waiting for a more diverse range of features and interactions.

Despite these limitations, Google is actively working on expanding the capabilities and accessibility of Gemini. As it evolves, users can anticipate a more inclusive and feature-rich integration within Bard, catering to a broader audience and diverse user preferences.

Google's ongoing efforts to improve and expand Gemini's capabilities for a more diverse range of features

Google's commitment to Gemini's evolution is evident in its ongoing efforts to introduce multimodal functionalities. This evolution will allow Gemini to seamlessly handle images, audio, and video, unlocking a new dimension of interactions and expanding user experiences.

Global Accessibility:

Recognizing the importance of global accessibility, Google is diligently working to overcome language barriers. Future versions of Gemini, particularly the upcoming Bard Advanced powered by Gemini Ultra, will support more languages than just English, making the technology accessible to a broader audience.

Beyond Text:

Gemini's trajectory is aimed at transcending its current text-based limitations within Bard. The upcoming Bard Advanced, utilizing Gemini Ultra, will introduce multimodal capabilities, enabling users to interact with a variety of media, including images, audio, and video.

Google's ongoing efforts to enhance and diversify Gemini's capabilities showcase a dedication to providing users with an increasingly sophisticated and versatile AI experience. As Gemini continues to evolve, users can anticipate a more inclusive and feature-rich AI interaction within the Google ecosystem.

Conclusion

In concluding our exploration of Google's groundbreaking Gemini AI, we find ourselves at the precipice of a new era in artificial intelligence. Gemini transcends the boundaries of its predecessors, emerging as a powerful and versatile large language model designed to reason seamlessly across text, images, video, audio, and code.

From revolutionizing computer vision to playing a pivotal role in geospatial science, human health, and integrated technologies, Gemini stands as a testament to the rapid advancements in AI capabilities. The introduction of AlphaCode 2 emphasizes its prowess in coding competitions, surpassing human experts and enhancing interactions across various applications.

Trained on Google's Tensor Processing Units (TPU), Gemini not only outpaces its predecessor PaLM in speed and cost-effectiveness but also sets the stage for the TPU v5p, a new system tailored for large-scale model training and execution.

The three variants of Gemini—Nano, Pro, and Ultra—cater to diverse user needs, with the Ultra variant undergoing safety checks and promising unparalleled capabilities in the near future. The integration of Gemini with Bard marks a significant improvement, paving the way for a future of rich and nuanced human-AI interaction.

While Gemini's journey with Bard is still in its early stages, with limitations in language support and geographical accessibility,

Google's ongoing efforts promise a more inclusive and feature-rich experience. The imminent launch of Bard Advanced, fueled by Gemini Ultra, signals a leap into multimodal interactions, supporting multiple languages and media types.

Gemini's impact extends to Pixel 8 Pro, where the Nano variant operates offline, enhancing Smart Reply and Recorder functionalities. The book has taken us through Gemini's evolution, its efficiency surpassing PaLM, and the significant role it plays in various domains.

As we look ahead, the ongoing evolution of Gemini promises a future where AI seamlessly integrates into our daily lives, offering advanced reasoning, understanding, and interaction across a multitude of tasks and applications. The journey with Gemini is only beginning, and the potential it holds for reshaping our digital landscape is boundless.

www.ingramcontent.com/pod-product-compliance
Lightning Source LLC
Chambersburg PA
CBHW071307050326
40690CB00011B/2556